Poems of
Passionate
Prayer

CARLISS M. FOREMAN

Poems of
Passionate
Prayer

CARLISS M. FOREMAN

Kravitz & Sons
INNOVATORS IN PUBLISHING, MARKETING AND ADVERTISING

Kravitz and Sons LLC
1301 Farmville Blvd, Suite 104
Greenville, NC 27834

Published by Kravitz and Sons LLC.

 ISBN: 979-8-89639-291-0 (sc)
 ISBN: 979-8-89639-292-7 (e)

Library of Congress Control Number: 2025916230

This book is dedicated...

To my Heavenly Father, who deposited this gift
in me for His glory! I thank Him for the
privilege and opportunity to share what he has
placed in my heart.

Acknowledgment

I thank God for my Pastors, Otis and Serena
Foreman, who have prayed and interceded,
blessed, encouraged, and supported my family
and me through the years. They
have been there for us through trials, tests, ups,
and downs and continue
to be a tremendous blessing in our lives! I thank
Him for my children and grandchildren.
My endeavor is to be a Godly example to them.

Introduction

We are living in the last days, where there are wars, rumors of war, death, destruction, famine, various diseases, and devastation everywhere.

In the Old Testament, God said he looked for a man to make up the hedge and stand in the gap, and he found none. Today, more than ever, God needs us to pray for each other.

Ezekiel 22:29-30

29. The people of the land have used oppression and exercised robbery and have vexed the poor and needy; yea, they have oppressed the stranger wrongfully.

30. And I sought for a man among them that should make up the hedge, and stand in the gap before me for the land, that I should not destroy it, but I found none.

I Timothy 2:1

1. I exhort, therefore, that first of all, supplications, prayers, intercessions, and giving of thanks be made for all men;

Contents

A Heart to Obey

Deuteronomy 11:26 Behold, I set before you this day a blessing and a curse; **Deuteronomy 11:27** A blessing, if ye obey the commandments of the LORD your God, which I command you this day:

Deuteronomy 11:28 And a curse, if you will not obey the commandments of the LORD your God, but turn aside out of the way which I command you this day, to go after other gods, which ye have not known.

1 Samuel 15:22 And Samuel said, Hath the LORD as great delight in burnt offerings and sacrifices, as in obeying the voice of the LORD? Behold, to obey is better than sacrifice and to hearken than the fat of lambs.

Acts 5:29 Then Peter and the other apostles answered and said, We ought to obey God rather than men.

Colossians 3:22 Servants, obey in all things your masters according to the flesh; not with eye service, as men-pleasers but in singleness of heart, fearing God.

A Heart to Obey

Father, your word declares to us
if we are willing and obedient
we shall eat the good of the land
I pray that we would embrace this word keeping
your statutes and commands
and a heart to obey
Obedience is better than sacrifice;
the word of God tells us so,
may our willingness to obey
help us to spiritually grow
When we choose to do our own thing,
we're rebelling against our master,
and the consequences of our actions
are destruction or disaster
Lord, give us the heart to obey
I pray for ears to hear instructions
and guidance along the way
I pray we do not get side-tracked
and begin to go astray
thank you for a heart to obey
May your perfect will be done in our lives
according to your precious word
may willingness and obedience
be the voice that we have heard;
we receive a heart to obey

Backslider

Luke 15:6 And when he cometh home, he calleth together his friends and neighbors, saying unto them, rejoice with me; for I have found my sheep which was lost.

Luke 15:7 I say unto you, that likewise, joy shall be in heaven over one sinner that repenteth, more than over ninety and nine just persons, which need no repentance.

Luke 15:10 Likewise, I say unto you, there is joy in the presence of the angels of God over one sinner that repenteth.

1 John 1:9 If we confess our sins, he is faithful and just to forgive us our sins and to cleanse us from all unrighteousness.

Backslider

Lord, I pray for the backsliders who have turned
their backs on you
they've become discouraged and hopeless and
don't know what to do
or they've decided to do their own thing seeking
only to please themselves
whatever the reason, dear God, I cry out to you
for help
I pray for their deliverance, restoration,
repentance, and healing
I pray they will learn to trust in you and not
depend on emotions or feelings
I pray that no matter what drove them away, be
it sin, offenses or pain
that they would forgive, forget and repent and
come home to the sheepfold again

Be Our Protection

Psalm 61:3 For thou has been a shelter to me, and a strong tower from the enemy.

Isaiah 43:2 When thou passest through the waters, I will be with thee; and through the rivers, they shall not overflow thee: when thou walkest through the fire, thou shalt not be burned; neither shall the flame kindle upon thee.

2 Thessalonians 3:3 But the Lord is faithful, who shall establish you, and keep you from evil.

1 Peter 3:12 For the eyes of the Lord are over the righteous, and his ears are open unto their prayers: but the face of the Lord is against them that do evil.

Be Our Protection

Father, I lift up all your people
in every city, state, and nation.
I pray for safety and protection
for all of your creation
I pray against hurt, harm, and danger
against the spirit of violence, rage, and anger.
Lord, be our protection
I pray against terrorism
and the threatening of lives.
I bind domestic violence
between husbands and wives
I pray for all children who are being abused;
help anyone and everyone who has been
misused
Lord, we need your protection
I pray for the elderly against break-ins or theft.
I pray against suicide and premature death
I pray that our President's life not be taken
and no other tragedy will cause lives to be
shaken.
God, thank you for your protection

Body Of Christ

Psalm 27:14 wait on the LORD: be of good courage, and he shall strengthen thine heart: wait, I say, on the LORD.

Psalms 31:24 Be of good courage, and he shall strengthen your heart, all ye that hope in the LORD.

Ephesians 6:10 Finally, brethren, be strong in the LORD and in the power of his might.

Ephesians 6:11 Put on the whole armor of God that ye may be able to stand against the wiles of the devil.

Body Of Christ

I pray for the body of Christ and
every brother and sister worldwide
now is not the time to be silent
nor the time to hide
God's word says to be bold and courageous to
stand for what you know is right
To put on the whole armor of God,
always prepared to fight
Don't be deceived or lulled to sleep;
don't let your guard down for a minute;
this walk is one of constant warfare,
and we're all engaged in it
We wrestle not against flesh and blood,
but principalities and wickedness too
the kingdom of God suffers violence,
so we must violently pursue
to take back what was stolen from us
or given by choices we made
it's by hearing and doing the will of God
that the enemy's hand is stayed.

Brother

Joshua 1:9 Have I not commanded thee? Be strong and of good courage; be not afraid, neither be thou dismayed; for the Lord, thy God is with thee whithersoever thou goest.

Isaiah 43:18 Remember ye, not the former things, neither consider the things of old.

Luke 17:3 Take heed to yourselves: if thy brother trespasses against thee, rebuke him; and if he repents, forgive him.

Ephesians 4:31 Let all bitterness, and wrath, and anger, and clamor, and evil speaking be put away from you with all malice:

Ephesians 4:32 And be ye kind one to another, tenderhearted, forgiving one another, even as God for Christ's sake has forgiven you

Brother

Lord, I pray for my brother
that we would grow closer together, and you
would bless our relationship, and with time it
would only get better
Though we may not always see eye to eye, we
sometimes argue and fight
my prayer is that you protect him and keep him
safe each and every night
May he grow closer to you
and get stronger with each new day; help him
hide your word in his heart and live in a Godly
way
In place of pride, he'd have humility leaning not
on his understanding or his own ability
Let him look to you, Lord Jesus, not to the
expectation of men
knowing that when life knocks him down, you
are there to help him up again

Business/Employers/Employees/Co-Workers

Joshua 1:8 This book of the law shall not depart out of thy mouth; but thou shalt meditate therein day and night, that thou mayest observe to do according to all that is written therein: for then thou shalt make thy way prosperous, and then thou shalt have good success.

Isaiah 48:17 Thus saith the LORD, thy Redeemer, the Holy One of Israel; I am the LORD thy God which teacheth thee to profit, which leadeth thee by the way thou shouldest go.

Romans 12:11 Not slothful in business; fervent in spirit; serving the Lord.

Colossians 4:1 Masters, give unto your servants that which is just and equal; knowing that ye also have a Master in heaven

Business/Employers/Employees/Co-Workers

Father, I pray for businesses employees and co-
workers too
I pray for employers and their staff, whether
temporary or part of a permanent crew
I pray for the peace of each office and all the
people working together for extra effort and
proficiency, each desiring to make things better
May each employee go beyond what's required
to help the company prosper and grow
and as they are faithful with another man's
things, you will bless the seeds they sow
I pray for peace and harmony with the
company's vision in mind. I pray against strife
and contention
and divisions of every kind

Cover Our Nations

Matthew 5:14 Ye are the light of the world. A city that is set on a hill cannot be hid.

Matthew 5:16 Let your light so shine before men that they may see your good works, and glorify your Father which is in Heaven.

Matthew 28:19 Go ye therefore, and teach all nations, baptizing them in the name of the Father, and of the Son, and of the Holy Ghost;

Mark 16:15 And he said unto them, go ye into all the world, and preach the gospel to every creature.

John 3:16 For God so loved the world, that he gave his only begotten Son, that whosoever believeth in him should not perish, but have everlasting life.

Cover Our Nations

I lift up every nation, each citizen of the same
for we're all a part of God's creation though too
numerous to name,
Lord cover our nations
I pray for every continent, each city large and
small, not overlooking anyone
I plead the blood over them all
I pray for the leadership of these nations to help
meet the people's needs
let them lead with hearts of compassion, not
with selfishness or greed
God, cover our nations
Keep them safe from harm and danger,
including the widow, the orphan, and the
stranger.
My prayer is for protection
provision and healthcare too,
God, I pray that every nation would rise up and
glorify you,
Father, cover the nations

Daughter

Psalm 32:8 I will instruct thee and teach thee in the way that thou shalt go: I will guide thee with mine eye.

Psalm 127:3 Lo, children are a heritage of the LORD: and the fruit of the womb is His reward.

Proverbs 22:6 Train up a child in the way he should go: and when he is old, he will not depart from it.

Proverbs 31:9 Many daughters have done virtuously, but thou excellest them all.

Daughter

Lord, I cry out to you for my daughter, deliver
her from worry and stress
I pray that she surrenders to you and finds true
joy and happiness.
I plead the blood of Jesus
over every area of her life
I take authority over confusion, fear,
discouragement, and strife. I see her as a woman
of God, virtuous and blessed
I pray that as she seeks your face, she finds
peace, contentment, and rest
May she look to you for guidance and strength
to run this race
help her dear God to persevere through the trials
she will face, and when she falls along the way,
encourage her to rise again
may she trust in you and be delivered from the
expectation of men

Enemies

Proverbs 16:7 When a man's ways please God, he maketh even his enemies to be at peace with him.

Proverbs 25:21 If thy enemy be hungry, give him bread to eat, and if he be thirsty, give him water to drink.

Luke 6:27 But I say unto you which hear, love your enemies, do good to them which hate you.

Luke 6:28 Bless them that curse you, pray for them which despitefully use you.

Luke 6: 35 But love your enemies, and do good and lend, hoping for nothing again, and your reward shall be great, and ye shall be children of the Highest, for he is kind unto the unthankful and the evil.

Enemies

Dear God, forgive my enemies; have mercy on
them too
they are my enemies through lack of knowledge
because they have no knowledge of you
I pray for their salvation Father, heal their
wounded heart
embrace them with your unconditional love,
and give them a brand-new start
Deliver them from bitterness, anger, and hatred
too, help them keep their heart and mind
focused on you. You said to pray for those who
use you,
curse you and speak evil things,
I pray that my enemies' minds are renewed and
see themselves as priests and kings

Father

Proverbs 17:6 Children's children are the crown of old men, and the glory of children are their fathers.

Proverbs 20:20 Whoso curseth his father or his mother, his lamp shall be put out in obscure darkness.

Malachi 4:6 And ye shall turn the heart of the fathers to the children, and the heart of the children to their fathers.

Ephesians 6:2 Honor thy father and thy mother, which is the first commandment with promise.

Father

My father in heaven, bless my father on earth,
give him strength and encouragement, too, and
with each new day
lead and guide him your way; help him lean and
depend on you.
Remind him that he is not alone
when the cares of the world get him down, you
will bring him through every trial and test
and keep his feet on solid ground
Society would have him be cold and hard no
feelings or emotions expressed
Let him know if he only surrenders to you,
he'll find peace, contentment, and rest. He's
called to be head of the house
to rule, guide, and protect
may his family give him the honor he's due with
mutual love and respect

Father-In-Law

Proverbs 17:6 Children's children are the crown of old men, and the glory of children are their fathers.

Malachi 4:6 And ye shall turn the heart of the fathers to the children, and the heart of the children to their fathers.

John 13:34 A new commandment I give unto you, that ye love one another; as I have loved you, that ye also love one another.

Colossians 3:23 And whatsoever ye do, do it heartily, as to the Lord, and not unto men.

Father-In-Law

I pray for the father-in-law of those who have
married
he has now gained a daughter or son
I pray the relationship this marriage has brought
will be a blessed and joyous one
I pray the father-in-law would open his heart
and welcome his child's spouse
and in turn, that daughter or son-in-law would
add laughter and joy to their house; whether
married for months or many years,
they've experienced trials and tests
my prayer is that the entire family will find
peace, harmony, and rest

Favor in the Famine

Job 10:12 Thou has granted me life and favor, and thy visitation has preserved my spirit.

Psalm 5:12 For thou, Lord, wilt bless the righteous; with favor wilt thou compass him as a shield.

Proverbs 3:4 So shalt thou find favor and good understanding in the sight of God and man.

Proverbs 8: 35 For whoso findeth me findeth life, and shall obtain favor of the LORD.

Favor in the Famine

Lord, I thank you for favor in the famine, and I
choose to love you rather than mammon
while all around me, things have dried up
my heart is full, and so is my cup because I
choose to walk by faith
and not by what I see or hear in the midst of the
famine
blessings have come from far and near.
You said to give, and it shall be given pressed
down and in good measure, and in turn, you've
blessed me with
the greatest of all treasure
You've entrusted me with distributing your
wealth, knowing I would do just that
and not hoard it for myself
I thank you for the strength and power that
helps me to stand fast
as I go through trials and tests, your word says
this too shall pass
as I look back over my life to reflect and
examine,
I want to thank you again, dear Lord
for favor in the famine

Five-Fold Ministry

Matthew 6:33 But seek ye first the kingdom of God, and his righteousness; and all these things shall be added unto you.

Ephesians 4:1 I, therefore, the prisoner of the LORD, beseech you that ye walk worthy of the vocation wherewith ye are called,

Ephesians 4:11 And he gave some apostles, and some prophets; and some, evangelists; and some, pastors and teachers;

Ephesians 4:12 For the perfecting of the saints, for the work of the ministry, for the edifying of the body of Christ:

Five-Fold Ministry

Lord, I pray for the five-fold ministry that you
gave to the body of Christ
some apostles, prophets, and evangelists for
which Jesus was sacrificed
The purpose of the five-fold ministry is to equip
us with your word
to compel us to do what it says and not just let it
be heard
How can we learn what God is saying except
there be a teacher
who will be there to confirm his word, except
there be a preacher
Lord, bless those you've called to this ministry
who has been faithful in answering the call,
having surrendered their own will
and have given to you their all

Fresh Anointing/Daily Bread

Psalm 23:5 thou anointest my head with oil; my cup runneth over.

Matthew 6:11 Give us this day our daily bread.

Luke 4:18 The spirit of the Lord is upon me because he hath anointed me to preach the gospel to the poor;

John 14:12 Verily, verily, I say unto you, He that believeth on me, the works that I do shall he do also; and greater works than these shall he do because I go unto my Father.

Acts 1:8 but ye shall receive power, after that the Holy Ghost is come upon you: and ye shall be witnesses unto me both in Jerusalem, and in Judea, and in Samaria, and unto the uttermost part of the earth.

Fresh Anointing/Daily Bread

Father, I pray for daily bread that, with your
word
our spirits may be fed
I pray for a fresh anointing to fill us and
overflow
consume us with Holy Ghost fire, then direct us
where to go
to spread your word and your love as evidence
of You in heaven above Father, this day we seek
your face
lead and guide us from place to place to share
the good news
to proclaim your word so throughout the land
the gospel is heard

Friends/Neighbors

Leviticus 19:16 Do not go spreading slander among your people. Do not anything that endangers your neighbor's life. I am the LORD.

Leviticus 19:18 Thou shalt not avenge, nor bear any grudge against the children of thy people, but thou shalt love thy neighbor as thyself: I am the LORD.

Proverbs 18:24 A man that hath friends must show himself friendly: and there is a friend that sticketh closer than a brother.

Proverbs 27:17 Iron sharpeneth iron; so a man sharpeneth the countenance of his friend.

John 15: 13 Greater love hath no man than this, that a man lay down his life for his friends.

Friends/Neighbors

God, you said if I want to have friends, then
friendly I must be
without any hidden motives, with true sincerity
You say to love in word and deed.
May I be a friend in time of need
I pray for strength to be there when tough times
come their way when we have disagreements
or hurtful things to say
I pray that you would bless them and keep them
safe from harm. Lord God, please be their
anchor when life brings them a storm
I pray for all my neighbors in safety; may they
dwell
I cover them in the blood of Jesus and pray that
all is well

Gifts of the Spirit

Malachi 3:12 And all nations shall call you blessed: and ye shall be a delightsome land, saith the LORD of hosts.

1 Corinthians 12:1 Now concerning spiritual gifts, brethren, I would not have you ignorant.

1 Corinthians 12:4 Now there are diversities of gifts, but the same spirit.

1 Corinthians 12:7 But the manifestation of the Spirit is given to every man to profit withal.

1 Corinthians 14:12 Even so ye, for as much as ye are zealous of spiritual gifts, seek that ye may excel to the edifying of the church.

1 Corinthians 14:40 Let all things be done decently and in order.

Gifts of the Spirit

Father, I pray on behalf of every believer
for a stirring of the gifts of the Spirit
so that when you speak to our hearts your
children will be able to hear it
The word of wisdom, the word of knowledge
working of miracles too
faith, healing, and prophecy
our spiritual gifts from you
divers tongues and interpretation
may we use these gifts to bless your creation;
let them be used for glorifying you
and not to exalt ourselves knowing that these
gifts are purposed
to bring help to someone else
as we yield to the spirit may the gifts just flow,
and the faith of your people grows and grows as
signs and wonders begin to manifest
all praise and glory to you, they will express

Healing/Wholeness

Isaiah 53:5 But he was wounded for our transgressions, he was bruised for our iniquities: the chastisement of our peace was upon him, and with his stripes, we are healed.

1 Peter 2:24 Who his own self bare our sins in his own body on the tree, that we, being dead to sins, should live unto righteousness: by whose stripes ye were healed.

3 John 1:2 Beloved, I wish above all things that thou mayest prosper and be in health, even as thy soul prospereth.

Psalm 103:3 Who forgiveth all thine iniquities; who healeth all thy diseases.

Healing/Wholeness

I pray for healing of body and mind of sickness
and disease
I pray against infirmity of every kind, from
headaches to feebleness of knees
I pray for the healing of heart attacks and
cancer.
I pray in Jesus' name because he is the answer.
I pray not just for healing but wholeness too
old things passed away; all things become new
because, by Jesus' stripes, we are healed
In the name of Jesus, all illness must yield
he was wounded for our transgressions, our
sicknesses he bore
be healed, be whole; you need not suffer
anymore

Intercessors/Prayer Warriors

Isaiah 65:24 And it shall come to pass, that before they call, I will answer; and while they are yet speaking, I will hear.

Matthew 7:7 Ask, and it shall be given you; seek, and ye shall find; knock, and it shall be opened unto you.

James 5:16 The effectual, fervent prayer of a righteous man availeth much,

1 John 3:22 And whatsoever we ask, we receive of him, because we keep his commandments, and do those things that are pleasing in his sight.

Intercessors/Prayer Warriors

Father, I pray for every intercessor who
sacrifices themselves in prayer
who stand in the gap and cry out to you for
mankind everywhere
who cries out for cities, states, and nations who
fervently pray for all creation
I lift them up with all their needs, their deep
concerns, and desires
I pray for fresh oil of joy and more Holy Ghost
fire as they get down on their knees
or lay prostrate on the floor as their prayers
reach your ears
may you bless them more and more.
I pray for those warriors
who boldly do battle in the spirit that each time
they pray for others, dear God, you would hear
it Protect them from all hurt and harm
keep them and their families safe and warm.
Lord, strengthen each prayer warrior
for victory in every situation
give them wisdom, knowledge, and
understanding
as they battle for all your creation

Loved Ones

Mark 11:25 And when you stand praying, forgive if ye have ought against any: that your Father also which is in heaven may forgive your trespasses.

Acts 16:31 And they said, believe on the Lord Jesus Christ, and thou shalt be saved, and thy house.

Ephesians 5:2 And walk in love, as Christ also hath loved us, and hath given himself for us an offering and a sacrifice to God for a sweet-smelling savour.

Galatians 6:10 As we have therefore opportunity, let us do good to all men, especially unto them who are of the household of faith.

Hebrews 10:24 And let us consider one another to provoke unto love and good works.

Loved Ones

Father, in the name of Jesus
I bring my loved ones before your face.
I pray for their salvation
and deliverance to take place all throughout our
family line from generation to generation
bring peace and love for each other most of all,
bring restoration
let us purpose to forgive and forget past hurts,
wounds, and pain
I pray that as each day goes by, we grow close as
a family again

Lust of the Eye/Lust of the Flesh/Pride of Life

Romans 12:1 I beseech you, brethren, by the mercies of God, that ye present your bodies a living sacrifice, holy, acceptable unto God, which is your reasonable service.

Romans 12:21 Be not overcome of evil but overcome evil with good.

Romans 13:14 But put ye on the Lord Jesus Christ, and make no provision for the flesh, to fulfill the lusts thereof.

1 Corinthians 3:16 Know ye not that ye are the temple of God, and that the Spirit of God dwelleth in you?

Lust of the Eye/Lust of the Flesh/ Pride of Life

Lord, I pray against the lust of the eye, the lust
of the flesh, the pride of life
I pray that your children would guard
themselves against evil, perversion, and strife
May our eyes be focused on holy things in the
natural and in the spirit
May our ears be tuned to the things of God so
that when gossip comes, we don't hear it
I pray our flesh would be put to death,
so, we don't let it overrule us
I pray against the spirit of pride because it can
surely fool us
let us not think more of ourselves than we really
ought
I pray for hearts of humility so that we can be
taught
to walk in purity and holiness,
be pleasing in God's sight
repenting of the wrong we've done and striving
to live upright.

Maintain the Marriages

Genesis 2:18 And the Lord said, it is not good that the man should be alone; I will make a help meet for him.

Genesis 2:24 Therefore, shall a man leave his father and mother, and shall cleave unto his wife; and they shall be one flesh.

Proverbs 18:22 Whoso findeth a wife, findeth a good thing, and obtaineth favor of the LORD.

Ephesians 5:22 Wives, submit yourselves unto your own husbands, as unto the LORD.

Ephesians 5:25 Husbands, love your wives, even as Christ also loved the church, and gave himself for it;

Hebrews 13:4 Marriage is honorable, and the bed undefiled: but whoremongers and adulterers God will judge

Maintain the Marriages

I pray for all marriages, each and every one
for those who've been together for years and
those who've just begun
Lord, maintain the marriages
I pray for seasoned marriages and newlyweds
and according to the word of God
I pray for undefiled beds. May the husband love
his wife
as God instructed him to
may the wife submit to her husband with the
respect that he is due
Father, maintain the marriages. May there be
laughter and romance, may the fire of their love
burn bright though they may argue and
disagree; let them lay down in peace each night
Bless and maintain the marriages
Let each spouse esteem the other higher
not needing to always be right, taking everything
to God in prayer to avoid having a fight
may happiness be a vital part of their life
together,
I pray they'll stay together forever
Lord, only you can maintain the marriages

Mothers

Psalm 113:9 He maketh the barren woman to keep house and to be a joyful mother of children.

Proverbs 20:20 Whoso curseth his father or his mother, his lamp shall be put out in obscure darkness.

Proverbs 31:26 She openeth her mouth with wisdom, and in her tongue is the law of kindness.

Proverbs 31:27 She looketh well to the ways of her household, and eateth not the bread of idleness.

Ephesians 6:2 Honor thy father and thy mother, which is the first commandment with promise.

Mothers

I pray multiplied blessings on mothers
everywhere, those we know as super moms
and those struggling with despair
I cry out for their health, endurance, and
strength
who, for the sake of their children
would go to any length
I pray for all young mothers who are trying to
cope, those who feel like giving up
Lord, let them know there is hope. Deliver them
from discouragement and fear
and give them the garment of praise so they
may be of good cheer
Bless that mother who has poured out her love
to the child, not from her own womb
but she labored hard in love and pain as she
opened her heart and made room
Bless each spiritual mother
who has embraced someone else's child as if
they were her own
even going the extra mile
God, give each mother rest and peace for what
she has and will go through; encourage her to
stand her ground, putting her trust completely in
you

Mother-In-Law

Colossians 3:13 Forbearing one another, and forgiving one another, if any man have a quarrel against you, even as Christ forgave you, so also do ye.

1 John 4:7 Beloved, let us love one another, for love is of God; and every one that loveth is born of God, and knoweth God.

1 John 4:11 Beloved, God so loved us, we ought also to love one another.

1 John 4:12 No man hath seen God at any time; if we love one another, God dwelleth in us, and his love is perfected in us.

Mother-In-Law

Mothers-in-Law are part of a family which can
make marriage hard to bear, so I lift my mother-
in-law up to you, Lord that my heart would be
just and fair
A mother-in-law does not want to let go of her
daughter or her son
which may not allow that marriage to grow and
the two to become one
your word says a man shall leave father and
mother and cleave unto his wife
this is not so easy to do
if there's jealousy, envy, or strife, Lord, I pray
that we can get along
and learn to love each other
I pray I can see her through your eyes and
embrace her as a mother

No More Addictions

Isaiah 61:1 The Spirit of the Lord God is upon me; because the Lord has anointed me to preach good tidings unto the meek; he hath sent me to bind up the brokenhearted, to proclaim liberty to the captives, and the opening of the prison to them that are bound.

John 8:32 And you shall know the truth, and the truth shall make you free.

John 8:36 If the son, therefore, shall make you free, ye shall be free indeed.

I John 4:4 Ye are of God, little children, and have overcome them: because greater is he that is in you than he that is in the world.

No More Addictions

Father, I pray against addictions of all kinds
of drugs, alcohol, things that alter the mind
I bind the spirit of perversion and lust.
I cry out to you, Lord your word I trust.
Lord, no more addictions
You said to cast our cares on you
we cast every care and pray for deliverance, too.
Whatever addiction have your people bound to
those things that bring torment and pain
I pray they are healed and restored as a whole,
never to be bound again
Lord, no more addictions
I come against fear, doubt, worry, and shame.
I take authority over addictions in Jesus' name
I pray for physical and emotional healing
I pray your people will be obedient and willing
to renew their minds by feeding on your word
by opening their ears so your word may be
heard,
Lord, no more addictions

Personal Business

Deuteronomy 8:18 But thou shalt remember the LORD thy God: for it is he that giveth thee power to get wealth, that he may establish his covenant which he sware unto thy fathers, as it is this day.

Psalm 1:1 Blessed is the man that walketh not in the counsel of the ungodly, nor standeth in the way of sinners, nor sitteth in the seat of the scornful.

Proverbs 3:9 Honour the LORD with thy substance and with the first fruits of all thine increase.

3 John 1:2 Beloved, I wish above all things that thou mayest prosper and be in health, even as thy soul prospereth.

Personal Business

Lord, I pray for personal businesses, those that
are birthed from home
May that business person know
that they are not alone, you have equipped them
with all the skills they need
to build a successful business that they can pass
on to their seed
let every client the business will serve receive the
honesty and integrity they deserve
whether a product to sell or a service rendered
may it be done as unto the Lord so that the
business is not hindered
I pray each business owner pays their tithes so
their business will be blessed
help them do what's right in the natural, and
you, Lord will do the rest

Presidents/Government

Isaiah 9:6 For unto us a child is born, unto us a son, is given: and the government shall be upon his shoulder: and his name shall be called Wonderful, Counselor, The Mighty God, The Everlasting Father, The Prince of Peace.

Isaiah 9:7 Of the increase of his government and peace, there shall be no end.

Joshua 1:5 There shall not any be able to stand before thee all the days of thy life; as I was with Moses, so I will be with thee: I will not fail thee, nor forsake thee.

Psalm 32:8 I will instruct thee and teach thee in the way which thou shalt go: I will guide thee with mine eye.

Presidents/Government

I pray and lift up all Presidents,
Prime Ministers, Kings, and Queens
I pray for the governmental body
that controls so many things
Let them lead their people
in a quiet and peaceful life
with more compassion and care,
less turmoil, and less strife
Strengthen our Presidents and government
to make the right decisions
give them wisdom and insight
when it comes to the country's provisions
bless the government body
of representatives, congressmen, mayors bless
senators and other officials
and cover them daily with our prayers

Prosperity

3 John 1:2 Beloved, I wish above all things that thou mayest prosper and be in health, even as thy soul prospereth.

Job 36:11 If they obey and serve him, they shall spend their days in prosperity and their years in pleasures.

Psalm 35:27 Let them shout for joy and be glad that favor my righteous cause: yea, let them say continually, Let the Lord be magnified, which has pleasure in the prosperity of his servant.

Psalm 122:7 Peace be within thy walls, and prosperity within thy palaces.

Prosperity

I pray for the prosperity of the soul and of
health
for spiritual riches and natural wealth
I pray for prosperity that money can't buy, such
as a broken heart mended
or an answer to a cry
I pray for prosperity of, happiness, and joy
that it may come to every girl and boy
and not stop there; let it go even further
so that it may reach every father and mother
I pray that it spreads to every city and nation.
I pray that it reaches all of God's creation

Raise up the Body of Christ

2 Chronicles 7:14 If my people, which are called by my name, shall humble themselves and pray, and seek my face, and turn from their wicked ways, then will I hear from heaven, and will forgive their sin, and will heal their land.

Proverbs 16:3 Commit thy works unto the LORD, and thy thoughts shall be established.

Matthew 6:33 But seek ye first the kingdom of God, and his righteousness, and all these things shall be added to you.

John 6:27 Labor not for the meat which perisheth, but for that meat which endureth unto everlasting life, which the Son of man shall give unto you:

For him hath God the Father sealed.

Raise up the Body of Christ

I pray for the body of Christ, especially in these
last days
Lord, help us to seek your kingdom and turn
from our wicked ways.
Raise up the Body of Christ
I pray that daily we come to you asking, Father,
what would you have me do
May the first thing we do when we open our
eyes is to thank You, Father, for allowing us to
rise Raise up the body of Christ
I pray the body of Christ would live in Godly
fear guarding our mouths, our eyes, and our
ears; stop looking to You for what we can get
but desire to have someone else's needs met
to stop being fearful of sharing your word
so that throughout the earth, the good news is
heard. Raise up the body of Christ
Let us go beyond the church walls and bring
God's word to the street by declaring the gospel
to everyone we meet. Please raise up the Body
of Christ

Salvation

Romans 5:8 But God commendeth his love toward us, in that, while we were yet sinners, Christ died for us.

John 3:17 For God sent not his son into the world to condemn the world; but that the world through him might be saved.

Romans 10: 9, 10 That if thou shalt confess with thou mouth the Lord Jesus, and shalt believe in thine heart that God hath raised him from the dead, thou shalt be saved. For with the heart, man believeth unto righteousness; and with the mouth, confession is made unto salvation.

Salvation

I pray for the salvation of those who are lost
who do not know Jesus as Lord and Savior.
I pray for not only a spiritual change
but a renewed mind and different behavior
that as they accept Jesus into their heart,
a radical change would take place
no longer desiring the things of this world
but desiring to seek his face
I pray they would be fruit that remains
and become disciples of Christ
that they, in turn, would lead someone else
to be saved and have eternal life

Schools/Teachers/Students

Matthew 5:16 Let your light so shine before men that they may see your good works, and glorify your Father which is in heaven.

Ephesians 4:15 But speaking the truth in love, may grow up into him in all things, which is the head, even Christ.

Philippians 1:10 That ye may approve things that are excellent, that ye may be sincere and without offense til the day of Christ.

2 Timothy 2:15 Study to shew thyself approved unto God, a workman that needeth not be ashamed, rightly dividing the word of truth.

Schools/Teachers/Students

Father, I pray for all students and teachers and
lift up to you every school
I pray for the faculty and all workers for every
regulation and rule
I pray for all school system's curriculum, and all
this entails
I pray for dedicated people so that sound
education prevails
I lift up all children in every grade level for
hearts open to learning all they can
I cry out for teachers and principals who are
willing to take a stand
I pray for teachers with compassion and a desire
to see children succeed and whose focus is
building their futures without selfishness and
greed
Lord, bless the needs of each educator with
recognition and an increase in pay for those
who go the extra mile
to keep each child from going astray
May the children be taught to dream and dream
big and believe that dreams do come true
if they work hard and persevere, there is nothing
they cannot do

Sister

Psalm 133:1 Behold, how good and how pleasant it is for brethren to dwell together in unity.

Acts 16:31 And they said, believe on the Lord Jesus Christ, and thou shalt be saved, and thy house.

Ephesians 4:32 And be ye kind one to another, tenderhearted, forgiving one another, even as God for Christ's sake hath forgiven you.

Philippians 1:3 I thank my God upon every remembrance of you.

Hebrews 10:24 And let us consider one another to provoke unto love and good works.

Sister

Father, I lift up my sister to you
I cover her in your precious blood to
keep her safe from hurt, harm, and danger;
deliver her from the spirit of anger
Heal every hurt, and her broken heart mend
protect it, so it doesn't get broken again
For the times we fought
or said unkind words
let that not make us drift apart
for although we may not always agree,
Lord, I love her with all of my heart
Bless her, Lord, for you know what she needs
and those things she may not express
help her to lean and depend on you
for peace, contentment, and rest

Son

Exodus 33:14 My presence shall go with thee, and I will give thee rest.

Psalm 127:3 Lo, children are a heritage of the LORD: and the fruit of the womb is His reward.

Proverbs 1:8 My son, hear the instruction of thy father and forsake not the law of thy mother.

Proverbs 3:5 Trust in the Lord with all thine heart, and lean not unto thy own understanding.

Revelation 21:7 He that overcometh shall inherit all things, and I will be his God, and he shall be my son.

Son

Father, I lift up my son to you
you know all the things he's gone through.
I pray that he looks to you for help
and does not try to carry the burdens himself.
He's a mighty man of valor,
a man after your own heart
I pray that he daily seeks your face and from
your word, he does not depart
When he feels discouraged, confused, or in
doubt
and not sure of what to do
Father, please show him there is a way out if he
will only put his trust in you
Don't lean on his own understanding or ungodly
advice from friends
I pray he seeks you for wisdom and guidance,
and on you only may he depend

Vision/Clarity/Manifestation

Habakkuk 2:2 And the Lord answered me and said, Write the vision, make it plain upon tables, that he may run that readeth it.

Habakkuk 2:3 For the vision is yet for an appointed time, but at the end, it shall speak, and not lie; though it tarry, wait for it; because it will surely come, it will not tarry.

Psalm 145:18 The Lord is nigh unto all them that call upon him, to them that call upon him in truth.

Isaiah 65:24 And it shall come to pass, that before they call, I will answer; and while they are speaking, I will hear.

Vision/Clarity/Manifestation

The word of the Lord says to write the vision
so that with it we may run
and let us clearly see his vision and the work
that needs to be done.
I pray that as the vision takes hold
in each of God's creation
it will move from the spiritual realm so that we
see the manifestation of whatever promises God
made to us since he's not a man to lie
will manifest here on this earth to be seen by the
human eye. If he said it, he would do it
what he has spoken is true.
I thank God for the vision and the
manifestation too

War/Troops

Psalm 23:4 Yea, thou I walk through the valley of the shadow of death, I will fear no evil: for thou art with me; thy rod and thy staff they comfort me,

Psalm 23:5 Thou preparest a table before me in the presence of mine enemies: thou anointest my head with oil; my cup runneth over.

Psalm 27:1 The Lord is my light and my salvation; whom shall I fear? The Lord is the strength of my life; of whom shall I be afraid?

Psalm 91:5 Thou shalt not be afraid for the terror by night; nor for the arrow that flieth by day;

War/Troops

Father, my heart cries out to you for our troops
engaged in war
I pray that the war will come to an end and the
fighting will be no more
I lift up every woman and man who has laid
down their lives
and has taken a stand
to fight for their country
and keep us safe
to sacrifice themselves
for the whole human race
I pray for each branch of the service army, navy,
and marines
I lift up the air force, too,
Lord; bless these precious beings
I pray for the families
of the troops that remain
in places where the war goes on
I pray they come home safe and whole
and the fighting is over and done

Widows/Orphans/Strangers

Deuteronomy 10:18 He doth execute the judgment of the fatherless and widow, and loveth the stranger, in giving him food and raiment.

Deuteronomy 27:19 Cursed be he that perverteth the judgment of the stranger, fatherless and widow. And all the people shall say Amen.

Job 29:13 The blessing of him that was ready to perish came upon me: and I caused the widow's heart to sing for joy.

Jeremiah 49:11 Leave thy fatherless children, I will preserve them alive, and let thy widows trust in me.

Widows/Orphans/Strangers

I pray for the widow, the orphan and stranger,
and those who are often neglected
that they would know joy, peace, and protection
and, with God, feel connected
no longer abandoned, abused, or deprived but
love as they've never known
so that they may know how precious they are
and never again feel alone
He is father to the fatherless his love for the
stranger is great. He tells the widow to trust in
him   and in him alone; she must wait
I pray they would feel a sense of belonging and
the love God has for them
and with each new day, they are given to live,
God draws them closer to Him.

Wisdom/Knowledge/Understanding

Ephesians 1:17 That the God of our Lord Jesus Christ, the Father of Glory, may give unto you the spirit of wisdom and revelation in the knowledge of him:

Proverbs 1:2 To know wisdom and instruction; to perceive the words of understanding

Proverbs 1:3 To receive the instruction of wisdom, justice, and judgment and equity;

Proverbs 1:5 A wise man will hear and will increase learning, and a man of understanding shall attain unto wise counsels:

Proverbs 1:7 The fear of the Lord is the beginning of knowledge: but fools despise wisdom and instruction.

Wisdom/Knowledge/Understanding

I pray for wisdom from Heaven above in every
area of your life
to live and move among all mankind in peace or
in the midst of strife
I pray that God gives you revelation knowledge,
both in the spiritual and natural realm
that you may know which way to go and your
life bring glory to Him
I pray God will give you understanding; without
it, you may go astray
but with wisdom, knowledge, and
understanding,
a solid foundation you'll lay

Conclusion

This book of prayer-poems was birthed out of the desire to pray for others. It's easy to pray on your own behalf or for your loved ones, but what about the co-worker you see every day, your neighbor who is suffering from domestic violence, or the backslidden believer?

How about the nations that are at unrest or that person suffering from sickness and disease, not to mention the unsaved person who needs to know the love, mercy, forgiveness, and eternal life that God wants to give them?

This is what prayer is all about. A call to make a difference in someone else's life through intercessory prayer. Before you begin to confess these prayers, ask the Holy Spirit to help you pray. Use these prayer-poems as a catalyst to launch you into passionate, fervent prayer that touches the very heart of Almighty God.

As you cry out on behalf of others, know that Jesus is sitting at the right hand of the Father, daily making intercession for you.

God bless each of you who will give yourself in prayer!

About the Author...

Carliss, whom God calls Hannah, a single mother of three children, was born in Beaumont, Texas, and currently lives in Los Angeles, California. She has been an intercessor for years. Her heart is to pray for God's people. He has gifted her with writing and blessed her to write this book of prayer poems to share with you.

About the Book...

As an intercessor (someone who prays for others), this book was birthed out of a desire to have prayer become a daily part of a believer's life. God calls us to pray for each other, and He does answer prayer. This book is written to encourage prayer by using prayer poems to help develop and build an effective, passionate prayer life!

www.ingramcontent.com/pod-product-compliance
Lightning Source LLC
Chambersburg PA
CBHW031229120626
46545CB00003B/1051